SUCCESSFUL SELF-MANAGEMENT

SUCCESSFUL SELF-MANAGEMENT

A Sound Approach to Personal Effectiveness

Paul R Timm

KOGAN PAGE

First published in the United States of America
in 1987 by Crisp Publications Inc, 95 First Street,
Los Altos, California 94022, USA.

This edition first published in Great Britain in
1988 by Kogan Page Ltd, 120 Pentonville Road,
London N1 9JN. Reprinted 1990.

British Library Cataloguing in Publication Data

Timm, Paul R.
    Successful self-management: a sound
    approach to personal effectiveness.
    1. Self-realisation – Manuals
    I. Title
    158'.1

    ISBN 1–85091–740–X
    ISBN 1–85091–739–6 Pbk

Typeset by DP Photosetting, Aylesbury, Bucks

Printed and bound in Great Britain by
Biddles Ltd, Guildford and King's Lynn

Contents

Preface

'Do more, do better and *do it faster*!' If we were to build a statue honouring modern society, that could be the inscription. The statue itself should be a racehorse – with blinkers. Fast and strong, but without the faintest idea where it's going. And after running as hard as it can, the horse ends up back where it started.

Do you sometimes feel like such an animal? You've trained, and you're ready to run for the rosettes, but you're not sure where the track is?

Most bookshops are loaded with titles on how to achieve that siren-goddess: 'SUCCESS', or how to achieve that management buzzword: 'EXCELLENCE'. But there is much the experts fail to tell us about the thrill of the chase, and the joy of reaching the inner contentment that tells you that you really are a person of worth, not another modern-day racehorse.

There are things we can do to take charge of our success. This book presents a sensible, logical, and psychologically sound way to apply those skills associated with human effectiveness. These include: time and task management, improved personal productivity, balance, and *life satisfaction*.

So take your blinkers off, and jump the rail. You're in for the time of your life as you master the keys to successful self-management.

Paul R Timm, PhD

PART 1: Getting Started

The following page contains an assessment which will get you started on the path to improved self-management. It is essential that you answer each question honestly. Since *Successful Self-Management* was designed as a 'do-it-yourself' book the only person affected by your answers and actions is you!

Where are you now?

Here are some important questions to get you thinking about where you are now. Answer each question honestly.

	Yes	No
1. Do you have a clear picture of where you are going in your professional life in the next five years?	( )	( )
2. Do others (ie, your supervisor/subordinates) know about your plans?	( )	( )
3. Have you set specific targets for your personal life for the next five years?	( )	( )
4. Do those you count on for support (family, close friends, etc) know about these targets?	( )	( )
5. Are you totally satisfied with the progress you are making in your professional life?	( )	( )
6. Are you satisfied with your personal life progress?	( )	( )
7. Do you have a written method of recording your professional and personal progress?	( )	( )

	Yes	No

8. Are your underlying values clear and sharp in ( ) ( )
   your mind?

9. Have you written them down? ( ) ( )

10. Do you sometimes feel guilty about successes ( ) ( )
    you have?

11. Are you as successful as you can be? ( ) ( )

Self-Management Defined

Your answers to the questions on page 11 can help to pinpoint opportunities for self-management improvement. The balance of this book is designed to help you convert these 'opportunities' for improvement into reality.

An acceptable definition of self-management would be:

Self-management is the *process* of maximising our *time* and *talents* to achieve *worthwhile goals* based on a sound *value system*.

Note the key words in this definition:

Process. Self-management is continuous. It is not something we do only once or occasionally. We make it a process by adopting some simple 'rituals' which will be taught in this book.

Time and **Talents.** These are unique personal resources which we alone can manage. In essence, this is all we have to offer and can really manage.

Worthwhile goals. These are the outcomes of our efforts – our planned-for achievements. To be truly worthwhile, such goals must be rooted in a sound value system.

Value system. Ultimately, we move towards that which we value. An understanding of our *personal* values is critical to the process of self-management.

As you work through this book, you will be taught the required skills to make the above definition of self-management a natural part of your life. In so doing, you will achieve even greater heights of psychological comfort and life satisfaction.

PART 2: Five Building Blocks to Success

The rest of this book will describe five 'building blocks'. Understanding and applying these concepts will allow you to develop the self-management skills necessary to become a more effective and confident person. The five building blocks are:

1. Understanding perspective

2. Understanding purpose

3. Understanding personality

4. Understanding planning

5. Understanding productivity

Block 1: Understanding Perspective

Perspective is our attitude to the amount of control we have over our lives. Some people feel helpless and overwhelmed by the demands the world seems to make on them. Others act as if they have virtually total *control* over every event that might affect them.

Let's think for a moment about this issue of personal control. I remember the first time I went skiing. My wife and I, both newcomers to the sport, visited a beautiful Swiss ski resort with friends. After an hour of slipping around and feeling awkward, our friends David and Judy patiently explained the basics (ie, how to stand up on skis and create the illusion that you've done all this before). Finally, they announced it was time to ride up our first lift.

It took only a few moments on the lift for a terrifying realisation to enter my mind. I noticed the lift seats were coming back down the mountain – empty. I also deduced that the lift never stopped to let people off! That meant that, like it or not, we were going to have to *ski* off the top of a mountain (to certain death, I was sure). Fortunately, my wife didn't put this all together until we were close to the top. Otherwise, she might have jumped early.

That is a feeling of having *no* control.

Unlike my wife and I on skis, most youngsters seem to enjoy forfeiting control. They eagerly hop on every ride at an amusement park. The more threatening the name of the ride, the better. The Maniacal Rodent, Terror Mountain, The Bone

Crusher – they love them all.

But as these same children become adults, rationality takes over. When cajoled (or tricked) into riding one of these things as an adult, they mentally conjure up every possible way the ride could crash and burn, and avoid staying on for more than the obligatory minimum.

Although we may be missing some 'fun' as we grow older, one factor underlies our conservatism: we really do want to stay in *control*. When we lack control of situations in which we find ourselves, we feel frustrated. In fact, a major source of occupational stress is the feeling of having too little control on the job.

Off the job, people increasingly find themselves adding to the number of balls they are trying to juggle. Career, family, community or religious activities, physical fitness, education, and other self-improvement efforts all take a bite out of our precious time and drain our limited energy. This, coupled with a 'do more, do better' psyche places considerable pressure on people. This is why many of us feel that our lives are out of control.

How do you look at control?

Take one minute and, in the box opposite, quickly write down a list of activities or events that you do control – any kind of event. When you have finished that list, take one more minute to list activities or events you cannot control.

Do you see any common characteristics in the items on the opposite page? Most people find that there are several things they cannot control and many of them have to do with *other people*. The activities in our lives that we can control usually have to do with *ourselves*. This leads to the simple conclusion that:

THE MOST FERTILE AREA FOR GREATER CONTROL LIES WITHIN OURSELVES

As you listed items in the chart on page 19 you probably felt some frustration because many events or activities in our lives do not neatly fit into the 'can' or 'cannot' control categories. A large number are 'grey area' events. We may be able to influence, or have some impact on these events – but do not or cannot

Activities or events I control	Activities or events I *cannot* control

absolutely control them. Likewise, sometimes we think we have more control than we actually do. The trick is to remain as realistic as possible.

For most events in life we can have *some* influence – but seldom will we have ultimate control. This applies especially to our dealings with other people.

A healthy perspective towards life-control may be summarised this way:
Life is a never-ending series of demands upon our time and talents. This 'stream' is constantly replenished by bosses, subordinates, family, friends, our sense of obligation, and our need to keep functioning. But for the successful life manager, the stream

is also replenished by his or her own dreams, goals, aspirations, and values. This type of replenishment becomes the *control* we use to influence the events of our life.

Self-check: How I allocate my time and talents

Tick yes or no beside each of the following statements to reflect how you act *as a general rule*. Be honest; don't show your answers to others.

	Yes	No	
1.	( )	( )	I spend most of my day doing what other people want me to do.
2.	( )	( )	I work on fun or pleasant tasks before doing the unpleasant ones.
3.	( )	( )	I wait until a deadline is near before really starting work on a project.
4.	( )	( )	I give high priority to those tasks that will advance my personal goals.
5.	( )	( )	I tackle jobs that can be completed in a short time before working on larger, longer-term tasks.
6.	( )	( )	I do the work which I've planned before doing the unexpected.
7.	( )	( )	I tackle the small jobs before embarking on the bigger ones.
8.	( )	( )	I work on the squeaky-wheel principle – the task that 'makes the most noise' gets worked on first.
9.	( )	( )	I wait to be told what to do first.
10.	( )	( )	I regularly think about how I am expending my efforts relative to my personal goals.

Self-check results

The self-check on page 20 may tell you something about your perspective on *control*.

If you answered Yes to items 1, 3, 8, or 9 you tend to be *reactive* to outside demand.. You wait until someone (or someone's deadline) pushes you to action.

If you answered Yes to items 2, 5, or 7, you may be acting upon *mistaken priorities*. Your decision to work on something appears to be because it looks easy or can be done quickly. People who do this regularly find themselves *tangled in the trivial* and seldom seem to have time or energy for what may be much more important.

If you answered Yes to items 4, 6, or 10, you are showing a *proactive* stance and are more likely to be in control. Saying Yes to these questions means you are moving towards successful life-management.

To be proactive is good, provided that you know where you are going. This brings us to our second success building block, *purpose*, which is described on the next page.

Block 2: Understanding Purpose

Our second success building block is *Purpose*. People without a sense of purpose lack focus in their lives. They are often guilty of *living by wandering around*, which may be the single most common cause of poor self-management.

Focus adds power to our actions. If somebody threw a bucket of water on you, you'd get wet, and probably cross too. But if water was shot at you through a high-pressure nozzle you might be injured. The only difference is focus.

Similarly the 'trick' to karate is that the entire force of a blow is centred in a very small area like the edge of the hand. That's why black belt karate experts can slam through a stack of boards without pain. They are *focused*. No mental or physical 'wandering around' here. Every fibre of a karate black belt's mind and body is concentrated, and the results are stunning.

When one author of the well known book *In Search of Excellence* was asked for 'one, all-purpose bit of advice' to help an organisation to achieve excellence, his response was:

Figure out your value system. Decide what your company stands for ... Put yourself out 20 years in the future: What would you look back on with the greatest satisfaction?*

The idea of a value system, for organisations *and* for individuals, is a powerful idea. Leading companies are aware of the power of

* Thomas J Peters and Robert A Waterman Jr, *In Search of Excellence* (London: Harper & Row, 1983).

a well defined value system. We should be also. The challenge to clarify values applies to leaders, not only in business, but also in community groups, church groups, families – and perhaps most important, to those of us interested in personal effectiveness and *self-management*.

A value is an idea of something that is intrinsically, in and of itself, desirable. To make it a personal value simply add the words 'to me'. Personal values need nothing else to justify their desirability, although we must be wary of issues that others may call values that are anti-social or destructive.

Once our value system is clarified, it will provide focus for our lives. By contrast, people or organisations that seem to have no direction are typically those without a coherent set of bone-deep beliefs. They tend to look only at results that can be easily measured. Value driven people and companies, on the other hand, express their core beliefs in *quality* terms such as customer satisfaction, innovation, personal growth, self-esteem, and life-satisfaction.

The most important concept any leader can bring to his or her organisation may well be an effort to clarify and breathe life into a value system. Once articulated, this system will provide a mission statement for leaders and followers alike.

How can we identify our value system? One interesting way to *begin* is provided in the worksheet on the next page.

Values worksheet

Mark each of the values listed below in one of the following ways.

Put a tick (✓) next to those values you personally *endorse*. These are values you would be willing to dedicate significant time and energy to achieve.

Put an X beside those values that you personally *reject*. These are values you would *not* be willing to expend much time or effort to achieve.

Put an 0 beside those values that are *neutral* to you – you neither endorse nor reject them.

Many of the values below may sound good to you. Force yourself to make some choices. Be honest about your willingness to dedicate a significant amount of time or effort to each. Do not show your responses to anyone.

I value ...

____ career success
____ honesty in all my dealings
____ religious activity
____ social correctness
____ open mindedness
____ high individualism
____ winning
____ ıny family's success
____ giving my children a competitive advantage
____ being law abiding
____ being loyal to country
____ orderly home life
____ keeping all commitments
____ knowing the right people
____ having balance in my life
____ having a wide range of friends
____ having many skills
____ being prepared for emergencies
____ athletic excellence
____ pride in my community, city, region
____ musical excellence

____ habits of thrift
____ financial wealth
____ self-sufficiency
____ involvement in government
____ marital harmony
____ fame within my profession
____ being productive
____ being creative
____ serving the less fortunate
____ health and vigour
____ keeping careful records
____ understanding other cultures
____ being a leader
____ mentoring others
____ intellectual growth
____ trust in God
____ financial security
____ personal attractiveness
____ tolerance of others
____ being witty, clever, articulate
____ artistic sensitivity
____ being a good team player
____ dressing for success

_____ awareness of my heritage

_____ projecting the right image

_____ honouring my parents

_____ ability to build things

_____ skill to influence

_____ skill to repair things or solve problems

_____ accuracy of work

_____ strong discipline

Rank the four values you endorse most strongly and the four you reject most vigorously:

MY TOP FOUR ENDORSED VALUES ARE	MY TOP FOUR REJECTED VALUES ARE
1.	1.
2.	2.
3.	3.
4.	4.

The exercise on this page is designed to start you thinking about values. Review the top four values you support and the four you reject most strongly and answer the following questions:

Yes   No

( )   ( )   Do you spend a major portion of your productive time moving towards agreement with your top four values?

( )   ( )   Do you spend time and effort moving towards acceptance of values you _reject_?

Identify one value conflict you noticed from this exercise. Can you pinpoint neutral or negative values where you are spending a disproportionate amount of time and effort? Are there other value areas where you should be doing more? In the box on page 26, suggest an action you could take to achieve better conformity with what you truly value.

Fine tuning your values

This page contains another exercise that can help to pinpoint your deep beliefs – your core values. Take a few minutes to answer these questions honestly. Don't show your answers to others.

1. What are your greatest professional and personal abilities and liabilities?

2. What are your most important goals for the current year?

3. What are your major professional or personal goals during the next 12 months? (Name two or three in each category.)

4. Twenty years from now, where will you live? What will you be doing? What assets will you own? What interests will you have? Will you be happy?

Values clarification

Below are some thoughts about values clarification:

1. Values are crucial to personal excellence
Personal effectiveness and balance require us to hold a set of clear

personal values. Without such bone-deep beliefs, we are much more likely to gallop off in different directions according to whim. Without values, self-management becomes little more than choosing from an array of equally worthy (or unworthy) activities. Without values it is easy to become subject to the 'tyranny of the immediate', and react to events rather than doing that which is most meaningful to us.

2. It isn't easy to sort out our values
If values clarification was an easy process, more people would do it. But it isn't, and they don't. One reason for the difficulty of the task is that values often present conflicts between two desirable goods.

For example, a worker may feel a greater need to maintain friendships by socialising with co-workers, than the need to finish his or her work. Another difficult choice is the question of allowing children the freedom to make personal choices, versus the high cost of their mistakes due to inexperience.

3. Values clarification must be put to work
Careful value planning takes time. This book will help to get you started, but the greatest benefit will come to those who spend hours on the *process* of value shaping.

One systematic way to do this is to set up a notebook or life planner that provides a place for you to write your core values and related activities.

The three-step value shaping process
Using a 'Life Plan Worksheet' similar to the one found in the Plan-It Life Organiser (page 29) let's work through an example of value clarification. Write your value shaping exercise on page 29, as you work through this exercise.

First, name a value that is important to you. Give it a name that you feel comfortable with. A good value area for example might be called *Health and Vigour*. Others could be *Financial security*, *Family*, *Leadership*, *Personal success*, *Spiritual growth* or *Balance*. You can add to this list.

Next, write the name of one value on your life plan worksheet

in the left column (see example below), and after you have
written the named value, then *describe* (using the present tense),
what it will be like when you are attuned to that value. In other
words, what will you be doing and thinking when you co-
ordinate with the value? Following is an example, using *Health and
Vigour* as a value.

plan·it life organizer	Life Plan
Core Values	**Value Aligning Activities**
HEALTH AND VIGOUR I exercise regularly and avoid harmful habits. I maintain reasonable weight. I get regular medical and dental checkups. I maintain vigour by daily planning, goal setting, and rewarding myself for accomplishments. I jog, play squash, swim, play golf, and occasionally do wild and crazy things to let off steam. I refuse to let stress grind me down. I avoid excessive worry. I view life as fun and full of opportunity.	• Jog 1000 + miles this year. • Get medical check up every 2 years • Have eyes checked every 3 years.

Although in the example, all descriptions were written in the
present tense, it is not necessary to have achieved them all yet.
For example, no one is able to avoid stress or excessive worry
always, and perhaps some activities (such as golf) are not played
regularly. But, putting descriptions in the present tense indicates
the direction that a person 'wants' to be going.

Here's another example, using the value heading *Financial
security*:

plan·it life organizer	Life Plan
Core Values	**Value Aligning Activities**
FINANCIAL SECURITY I can afford all that I need, as well as some luxuries. I take a holiday each year. I have no debts; even my home is paid for. My income is secure. I have a plan for my retirement, adequate insurance, etc. I have a good income — productive shareholdings. We are comfortable but not extravagant.	• Save 10% of earnings • Buy £5,000 worth of Blue Chip Ltd by Jan. • Review life insurance this year. • Pay off car loan within 18 months.

plan·it life organizer	Life Plan	
Core Values	**Value Aligning Activities**	

Summary of the three steps in basic value shaping
1. Name the value
2. Describe what it feels like to be in conformity
3. Describe value-aligning activities – (which is the next part of this book).

Value aligning activities
(or the comfortable marriage of values and goals)

The ancient philosopher, Seneca, said:

> Our plans miscarry because they have no aim. When a man does not know what harbour he is making for, no wind is the right wind.

Much has been written about goal setting. We have all heard the familiar litany: set short- and long-term goals, concentrate on them, direct your energies towards their accomplishment, and you will enjoy *success*.

Goal setting is a motivational technique that works – it is not a fad. As one textbook which surveyed the research on goal setting concludes, 'In business and in life, goal setting is a uniquely powerful tool for increasing productivity.'*

But why does it work? Perhaps the best reason is because goals give direction to life. They provide points of reference.

This book differs from most other goal setting books because it maintains that *the base of any goal must harbour an anchoring value*.

If an individual sets the following goals, for example:

1. Jog 20 miles each week
2. Take both of the children out this month, and
3. Average 10 sales calls each day,

what might be the underlying values?

---

* Edwin A Locke and Gary P Latham *Goal Setting: A Motivational Technique That Works!* (Englewood Cliffs, NJ: Prentice-Hall, Inc., 1984, quoted from dustcover.)

Write your answers in the spaces below.

1. _____

2. _____

3. _____

Author's commentary

The jogging goal on page 30 would probably be anchored in a value called *health*; the 'date with kids' goal would be based in a value having to do with *family*; and the sales call goal probably would find its root in a *career* value.

Goals often relate to several, interconnected values. The 'sales call' goal can be based in *financial, personal growth*, or even *social* values.

Having a personal value system can be visualised as the foundation of a building. The building itself (ie, personal goals and activities) will be structurally sound only to the extent that the foundation is solid.

Failure to create a link between goals and their values runs the risk of working towards goals which have no attachment to personal values. Such goals are hollow. Good goals have several characteristics that are common. They are listed below.

Characteristics of good goals

Effective goals – the kind that really do motivate – should:

- Be concrete and specific – phrased in a way that is clear.

- Be realistic – they should stretch us, but not beyond the bounds of what is reasonable.

- Be measurable in some quantitative and/or qualitative way.

- Include deadlines.

- Be value anchored.

- Be *written*. An unrecorded goal is only a wish.

Go back to the life plan worksheets on page 29. In the column to the right of the 'Core Value' is where you will write your 'Value Aligning Activities'. For each value you have described on the worksheets, write several 'Action Targets' (goals) which will help you to achieve oneness with your value.

For example, look at the HEALTH AND VIGOUR value on page 28. The individual has written in the 'Value Aligning Activities' column that he/she will jog at least 1000 miles per year, get a complete physical check-up every two years, and have his/her eyes checked every three years.

In similar fashion, the FINANCIAL SECURITY value example (page 28) is accompanied by the following 'activities': save 10 per cent of all earnings; buy £5,000 worth of Blue Chip Ltd stock by January; review life insurance coverage every three years; and pay off car loan within 18 months.

Every goal-seeking activity in the above example is anchored in a value. The value clarification process helps to make purposeful goals, and these goals provide the motivation to achieve success.

Herein lies the productive marriage of values and goals.

If it isn't written down, it isn't a goal
People in my seminars say, 'I have lots of goals, I just haven't written them down.' My reaction is that if a goal isn't written down, it isn't a goal – it's a wish. Occasionally wishes come true, but not as often as goals.

Block 3: Understanding Your Personality

The third building block is *Personality*. Specifically, two aspects of personality that most affect the success of an individual are:

1. Assertiveness

2. Receptiveness

Both of these will be discussed in this section. By committing yourself to better self-management you are taking charge, and avoiding the pitfalls of having others hold you back.

Assertiveness

Let's look first at assertiveness which can be defined as *being pleasantly direct*.

With an understanding of *Control* (Block 1) and a clearer value system and *Focused goals* (Block 2) you are now ready to make better decisions about the use of your time and talent. When faced with requests (or demands) to do something that runs against your plan, by understanding assertiveness, you'll have the ammunition you need to say the most important word in any self-manager's vocabulary: *No*.

How assertive are you?

By answering the following questions honestly, you will better understand your attitude towards assertiveness. An attitude, of course, does not always show up in behaviour. You may *feel* more assertive than you *are* in real-life situations.

Circle T (true) or F (false):

1. T F I often feel like telling people what I really think of them.

2. T F When I find myself in a new situation, I watch what other people do and then try to act in a similar fashion.

3. T F I enjoy doing things that others may regard as unconventional.

4. T F I think it is important to learn obedience and practise correct social behaviour.

5. T F In general, I find that I dislike non-conformists.

6. T F I prefer to listen to the opinion of others before I take a stand.

7. T F I feel comfortable following instructions and doing what is expected of me.

8. T F It often makes more sense to go along with 'the group' rather than try to persuade them to my point of view.

9. T F Confronting other people is extremely uncomfortable for me.

10. T F I enjoy being seen as a person with strong opinions.

SCORING YOUR ASSERTIVENESS QUIZ

If you answered True to items 2, 4, 5, 6, 7, 8, or 9, above give yourself one point for each. Also give one point for False answers to items 1, 3, or 10, and total your points.

If you scored 6 or more points, low assertiveness may be a problem for you. You may find yourself being far more reactive to the demands of others than you are to your own aspirations.

Many excellent books are available that can help develop one's assertiveness. Read some of this material and try some new, more assertive behaviour.

How receptive are you?

RECEPTIVENESS means fishing for feedback. Obtaining feedback, even from your most severe critic, may be the most important way for you to gain direction and control. This feedback can lead to greater self-management effectiveness. Read the following case, and respond to the questions.

While jogging with his good friend Bob the other day, Bill got on the subject of corrective criticism. Bob confided to Bill that he was having difficulty understanding why his relationship with his girlfriend didn't seem to be going anywhere.

'If only she'd say what it is about me that doesn't appeal to her, I'd work on changing,' Bob said, 'but she just won't say. You're an old friend, Bill. What do you think I'm doing wrong?'

Bill had been waiting for this. Bob is a really good guy, but does have some irritating traits. For example, he's extremely competitive. So, what the heck, Bill thought, I'll tell him now while he seems to be looking for feedback.

'Bob,' Bill began, 'You do have one trait that I find irritating, and maybe it bugs your girlfriend too. You are the most bloodthirsty, competitive person I've ever met.'

There was no response and Bill thought Bob didn't seem too

upset by what had just been said, so he continued: 'In fact, whenever we play squash it isn't even fun. You're so intense, you can't even say "nice shot" when I hit one. To be honest with you, Bob, you'd be a lot nicer to be around if you'd be a little more charitable with your compliments.'

Bill was in full flight: 'In fact, Bob, I'd much rather play against Brent. Every game doesn't seem like life or death to him. And he's forever saying "great shot" and still equable after the game, even if you beat him. He even lets up once in a while if you're really having a miserable game and ...'

Suddenly, Bill realised that Bob wasn't responding. He wasn't getting angry. He also wasn't even thoughtfully considering the 'constructive criticism'. In fact he was laughing out loud.

Bob said, 'Bill, do you realise that you just described perfectly, *your* style on the squash court? That's *exactly* why I get frustrated playing against *you*.'

Bill stifled his reaction. He wanted to give Bob 'Oh yeah, says who ...' when light dawned. Bob was right. After a moment, Bill started laughing too.

Questions

1. What do you feel is the primary message of this case?

_____

_____

_____

2. Do you think Bill's observation was correct?

_____

_____

_____

3. Do you think Bob's response was appropriate?

_____

_____

_____

4. Is there a message here that you can personally relate to?

_____

_____

_____

Feedback receptiveness quiz

Answer the questions as honestly as possible. Do not show anyone your answers.

As a general rule:

	Yes	**No**	
1.	( )	( )	I get embarrassed when people point out my mistakes.
2.	( )	( )	I resent people telling me what they think of my shortcomings.
3.	( )	( )	I regularly ask friends and associates I trust to comment on how I'm doing.
4.	( )	( )	I know how to offer constructive criticism to others in a sensitive way.
5.	( )	( )	I like people who tell me their reactions to my activities because it will help me adapt my behaviour in future.

Author's comments on feedback receptiveness

If you answered a definite Yes to items 1 and 2 you may be putting up some attitude barriers that could deter you from obtaining useful feedback. We are normally uncomfortable when we receive harsh or insensitive feedback, but even that can be valuable, if we take it in perspective. Even our worst critic can provide a 'gift' of good advice, if we don't allow the emotion of the moment to blind us. Successful people learn how to develop an attitude of looking for a gem of good advice even when it's buried under a lot of worthless noise.

If you answered Yes to items 3 and 4 you are creating a climate where helpful feedback is accepted and expected. Organisations fostering such a climate are typically positive places to work and successful in their results. In a similar fashion, individuals who foster a 'receptive' attitude receive the benefit of input from others.

If you answered Yes to item 5, you are probably a little unusual. But you're on the right track.

We never really do know how we are coming across to others unless we seek *feedback*, and realise that feedback is a critical ingredient of successful life-management.

Feedback in business

An unhappy customer can be a business's best friend. Feedback is critical to an effective business. One study indicated that dissatisfied customers tell, on average, ten other people about their dissatisfaction. About 20 per cent of such people tell 20 or more people. Also, it has been proved that it costs seven to ten times more to gain a new customer than to keep an existing one.

The most interesting fact is that even the most dissatisfied customers who receive an indication that their complaint has been heard and acted upon, *do* come back. The most dangerous situation is when there are unhappy customers who do *not* tell the company of their dissatisfaction. In a sense then, an unhappy customer is a company's best friend *provided the company gets feedback*. Because of this, enlightened companies go to great lengths to make it easy for customers to comment about service.*

* For an excellent book dealing with this subject, read *Customer Service* (Kogan Page).

This same principle can apply to our daily interactions with friends, associates and business contacts.

Feedback receptiveness is an attitude
Less successful companies *and* people prefer to be ostriches. They bury their heads and tune out all negative comments. In so doing, they refuse to be teachable. Confirming and clarifying how we are relating to others requires feedback from those with whom we deal. Feedback becomes the control system of our self-management.

Complete the following sentence in your own words:
I plan to encourage useful feedback by ...

_____

_____

_____

_____

_____

How to nurture good feedback

For most people, giving criticism (even when done in a constructive way), is a risky business. When people first do it, they watch very closely to see what happens. The reaction they receive will usually determine whether such feedback is offered again. This means that you have an opportunity to avoid turning off future feedback if you do the following:

1. Stay non-defensive. Listen – don't explain or justify
Learn to bite your tongue. When feedback is being offered is not the time to explain or justify your actions (even if you feel the

criticism is unwarranted or stems from a misunderstanding). When you request feedback, the burden is on you to listen and try to understand. This does not mean you are obliged to believe or accept the information, but it does allow you to try to understand why the other person feels and reacts the way he or she does. Defensiveness will stifle feedback. It tells the other person that you are more interested in justifying yourself than in understanding what is being said.

2. Ask for more information, especially specifics
When you are engaged in a feedback session, there is an opportunity to obtain additional information. If you can honestly keep saying, 'That's extremely helpful. Tell me more. Is there anything else I should know about that?' it will support and encourage a continual flow of feedback.

3. Express an honest reaction
The person giving the feedback wants to know your reaction to the information being presented. The best guideline is to express your honest reaction. 'I'm a little surprised you said that but you probably have a point,' or 'I'm not sure what to say. I never even thought of that, but I will from now on.'

4. Thank those providing feedback and plan for the future
Let people know that you realise how risky giving criticism can be, and show your appreciation for their efforts. This might also be a good time to plan for future sessions. These should be less disturbing and more productive than the first one, because you have proved your receptiveness. Most excellent leaders make this process a regular and continuing one.

Having said all that about feedback, you should realise that not many people are able to handle the four points presented, not because they wouldn't benefit from it, but because they are afraid to hear it. *It takes a lot of courage not only to hear criticism, but actually to request it!* It is very common to see other people avoid reality by keeping their heads comfortably planted in the sand.

The highly successful person is willing to do what the unsuccessful person is not. Getting feedback in order to provide direction and control is a classic example of such an action. When you learn to do it, you'll reap a rich reward.

Feedback checklist

Think back to the last time you received criticism from someone else. Did you:

Yes   No

( )   ( )   Avoid defending or explaining yourself until the full criticism was expressed?

( )   ( )   Understand the criticiser's point of view as best you could?

( )   ( )   Ask for elaboration or clarification?

( )   ( )   Express an honest reaction?

( )   ( )   Thank the person for the feedback?

Is your future behaviour regarding feedback likely to change?

Yes   No

( )   ( )

Block 4: Understanding Planning

Planning is the fourth building block to successful life management, *and it is critical to your success.* This block is where you actually write out specifics for your daily activities.

The nuts and bolts of time and task management

Most time management experts agree that rule number one in a thoughtful planning process is: *Use some form of planner where you can write things down.* The author of this book has designed a format called the <u>Plan-It Life Organiser</u>© (you saw a sample 'Life-Plan' page earlier). In the next few pages, you will see other sample pages from the <u>Plan-It</u>© material. You may prefer to construct your own planner system or use another published format.

How much time should you devote to daily planning? It will vary with each individual, but a minimum of 10 or 15 minutes a day devoted solely to planning is recommended. Use the steps described below and you should see a significant increase in your personal effectiveness.

How to do effective daily task planning

To use the sample planner sheet (page 45) effectively, practise applying the following steps. See page 44 for an example of a completed planner sheet.

1. Develop a priority task list for each day
Prioritising tasks helps us to sort them out, decide which need to

be attacked first, and which can be saved for later.

Here's the process: list in your planner the specific tasks you want or need to spend your time on that particular day. Use your own 'shorthand' (provided you can recognise it when you read it later). List the items (ie, 'Complete the XYZ report', 'Get stamps', 'Attend Billy's softball game', 'Eat more fish', or 'Keep date' with wife, husband or child).

Don't be over concerned with the *importance* of the items at this stage, just get into the habit of listing all non-routine tasks that you want to accomplish that day.

2. *Assign a letter priority to each item on your list*

Use **A, B, C,** or ★ (star) and put the letter **A** next to items that *must* be done. These are critical to you. You alone determine whether they are critical or not. This decision is based on your values and goals. Tasks required either by outside forces (like your boss) or internal ones (such as a personal commitment) will normally receive an **A** priority. In <u>Plan-It</u>, place the letter in the column right next to the item. Put the letter **A** for *must do* items.

Use the letter **B** to indicate *should do* items. These are things that should be done, those items that are really worth spending some time on. They aren't quite as critical as the **A**s, but they're nevertheless important.

The letter **C** is for *could do* items. These are things worth listing, and worth thinking about. And if you get the **A**s and **B**s completed, worth doing.

A star ★ indicates an item that is *urgent* – something that *must* be done *now*! It is both important and vital. You've got to get on to it right away. These items occasionally come up during a working day (ie, a crisis). When you add them to your list, put a star by them, and drop whatever else you're doing, even if it's an **A** item – and complete that task.

Use a star very sparingly. Urgent tasks are normally not planned during your dedicated planning time. They pop up and scream 'do me now!' Be careful, however, to decide that an item really is important before you bump the rest of your plan to squeeze it in. Just because something makes a lot of noise doesn't mean it necessarily has to be done instantly. Don't let an apparent urgency override a planned *important* task.

3. *Assign a number to your tasks*

You can further sharpen your plan of attack by assigning a number to each task.

Use the numbering system as a chronological indicator. That is, ask which task should you realistically do first. If you have a meeting at two in the afternoon and it's an **A** item, it may not be **A-1**, simply because there are other things to do earlier in the day. As with other priorities, you decide how best to use it, but a number system will provide your marching orders.

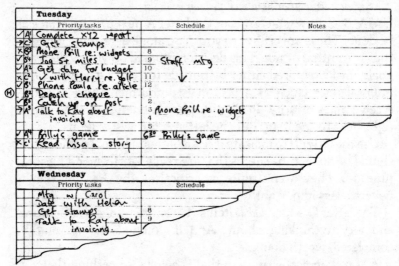

Assume that tomorrow is Monday. Go through the three steps on pages 42–4, and begin listing and prioritising what you really need to do 'tomorrow'. Include both business and personal tasks – especially those which tie in with your core values. Write your plan on the form shown on the facing page.

Completion symbols: the pay-off

As you complete the tasks listed in your planner, you deserve a reward. This reward takes the form of a completion symbol.

Here are several completion symbols, starting with one that feels the best:

plan·it life organizer	Week of 19	This week		

A	Must do	✓	Completed
B	Should do	→	Moved
C	Could do	( )	Delegated
★	Urgent – DO NOW	✗	Deleted

Monday

Priority tasks	Schedule	Notes
	8	
	9	
	10	
	11	
	12	
	1	
	2	
	3	
	4	
	5	
		✓ Journal ⃞

Tuesday

Priority tasks	Schedule	Notes
	8	
	9	
	10	
	11	
	12	
	1	
	2	
	3	
	4	
	5	
		✓ Journal ⃞

Wednesday

Priority tasks	Schedule	Notes
	8	
	9	
	10	
	11	
	12	
	1	
	2	
	3	
	4	
	5	
		✓ Journal ⃞

(✓) The tick symbol indicates the task has been completed. That, my friends, should feel good. Many people prefer to put their ticks all in red as a reminder of just how productive they have been.

(→) A second symbol, an arrow, is used when a task needs to be rescheduled, (for whatever reason). Perhaps a meeting has been cancelled or an appointment changed, or it simply could not be completed because you were wrapped up in something else.

Important. Any time you use the arrow, be sure to reschedule the task to another day in the planner. When you use that arrow and reschedule the task for another day, you earn the right to forget about it for a while. You'll be reminded automatically on the new day you scheduled. And it'll be there when you do your daily personal planning.

(Ⓗ) A third symbol often used is a circle which is placed in the margin to the left of the completion symbol column. This symbol indicates the task has been delegated to someone else.

It may be that you've asked your spouse to pick up a book of stamps on the way home from work, or assigned a child to clean out the garage. Or it may be a more formal kind of delegation, where you've given a colleague or subordinate a task to complete. If you have several people reporting to you, you may want to use the circle and put the initial of the person to whom the task has been delegated inside the circle. When the task has been completed by that person, you should then put a tick in the 'completed' column.

(X) A fourth symbol is an X, which simply means that a task has been deleted. It may mean that you blew it and it just didn't get done, or it may mean that you've reconsidered and determined that this task simply isn't worth doing. Remember, you are in charge. If you schedule a task but later decide it really isn't what you want to do – so be it. You (X) it out.

To review the priority codes and completion symbols, write in what the symbols below mean. If you are uncertain, read the material just presented.

A =   ✓ =

B =   → =

C =   ○ =

★ =   X =

Tying goals and values to your daily planning

Your priority task list should provide a micro view of your daily activities. But how do these activities tie in with those long-term values and goals we've been talking about?

For a majority of people, they *don't*! And that's why people often fail to achieve what's really important to them. The challenge is to *make your daily activities consistent with your goals and values.*

The Plan-It Life Organiser contains three sections which provide special tools to help you be successful:

1. A monthly plan section

2. A yearly plan record

3. Your life plan.

A sample of each of these pages can be seen beginning on page 52.

While doing your daily priority task planning, work to make sure that the goals and values you previously articulated for yourself are evident. The 'life plan' section of a planner is where you *record your core values, and your value aligning activities.* It is important to refer to them. The more often these are reviewed, the more likely they will become a part of your being. Your daily plan should reflect 'the big picture' described in your life plan.

Likewise, your yearly plan, and monthly plan, should promote specific *tasks* relevant to your daily *activities*. For example, if your life plan indicates a high value for 'health and vigour', you have probably created value aligning activities, such as a regular exercise programme of jogging or aerobics. For your yearly plan record, a priority task might be that you're going to jog 500 miles, or exercise in an aerobics class at least three times each week for the calendar year.

You then translate your targets into a task of jogging 40 miles, or attending 12 aerobic sessions this month. This goal should be entered on your monthly plan page. Since you have decided that you want to run or exercise a specific amount during a month, it is simple to translate the monthly goal into daily objectives. So your priority task for a particular day may be to run three miles or attend an exercise class. When you write that down, you have translated your values and long-term goals into daily targets. You have learned to focus your energy on completing those individual tasks which relate to much larger life goals.

Translate one of your core values into a daily activity in the exercise below. First write one of your core values in the top space. Then work your way down to daily activities as indicated:

_____	CORE VALUES	'One of my lifetime goals'
_____	YEARLY EVENTS	'What do I want to accomplish this year towards that core value?'
_____	MONTHLY EVENTS	'What do I need to accomplish this month on my yearly objective?'
_____	WEEKLY EVENTS	'What do I need to accomplish this week on my monthly goal?'
_____	DAILY EVENTS	'What do I want to accomplish today to bring me in line with the above lifetime goal?'

Plan-It forms

The next six pages are taken from the Plan-It Life Organiser©. To be successful in the area of self-management will require some sort of personal planner.

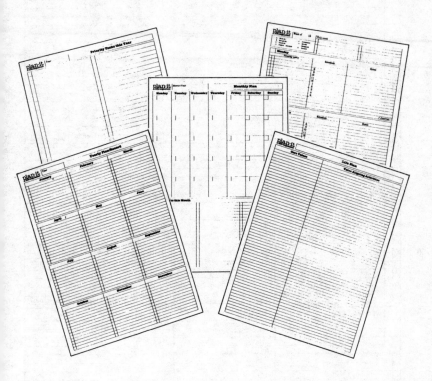

© Paul R Timm

plan·it life organizer | Week of ____ 19 ____ | This week

A	Must do	✓	Completed
B	Should do	→	Moved
C	Could do	··	Delegated
★	Urgent DO NOW	✗	Deleted

Monday

Priority tasks	Schedule	Notes
	8	
	9	
	10	
	11	
	12	
	1	
	2	
	3	
	4	
	5	

✓ Journal [ ]

Tuesday

Priority tasks	Schedule	Notes
	8	
	9	
	10	
	11	
	12	
	1	
	2	
	3	
	4	
	5	

✓ Journal [ ]

Wednesday

Priority tasks	Schedule	Notes
	8	
	9	
	10	
	11	
	12	
	1	
	2	
	3	
	4	
	5	

✓ Journal [ ]

Thursday

	Priority tasks	Schedule	Notes
		8	
		9	
		10	
		11	
		12	
		1	
		2	
		3	
		4	
		5	
			✓ Journal □

Friday

	Priority tasks	Schedule	Notes
		8	
		9	
		10	
		11	
		12	
		1	
		2	
		3	
		4	
		5	
			✓ Journal □

Saturday

	Priority tasks	Schedule	Notes
			✓ Journal □

Sunday

	Priority tasks	Schedule	Notes
			✓ Journal □

plan·it life organizer	Month/Year	Monthly Plan				
Monday	**Tuesday**	**Wednesday**	**Thursday**	**Friday**	**Saturday**	**Sunday**

Major Tasks this Month

plan·it life organizer	Year	Yearly Plan/Record	
January		**February**	**March**

April	**May**	**June**

July	**August**	**September**

October	**November**	**December**

plan·it life organizer	Year	Priority Tasks this Year

plan·it _{life organizer} Year	Priority Tasks this Year

plan·it
life organizer

Life Plan

Core Values	Value Aligning Activities

Block 5: Understanding Productivity

The last 'P' of our success building blocks is *Productivity*, which is the measure of successful self-management. Six of the most common productivity killers are given below. In the space provided, list two or three defences you can use against each. Beginning on page 58 are some additional ideas you may not have considered.

Productivity killer   **What do you do to defend against this killer?**

1. INTERRUPTIONS   _____

    Is this a problem for you?   _____

    ( ) Yes   ( ) No   _____

2. CLUTTER and
    PAPERWORK   _____

    Is this a problem for you?   _____

    ( ) Yes   ( ) No   _____

3. UNPRODUCTIVE
    COMMUNICATION   _____

    Is this a problem for you?   _____

    ( ) Yes   ( ) No   _____

4. PROCRASTINATION   _____

   Is this a problem for you?   _____

   ( ) Yes   ( ) No   _____

5. INDECISION   _____

   Is this a problem for you?   _____

   ( ) Yes   ( ) No   _____

6. SELF-OVERLOAD   _____

   Is this a problem for you?   _____

   ( ) Yes   ( ) No   _____

Time-tested defences against productivity killers

INTERRUPTIONS

1. Assertively decline to be interrupted
The next time someone asks, 'Have you got a minute?' you may be wise to gather up your most assertive skills (which doesn't mean being abusive or abrasive) and simply say, 'No, I really don't. I'm in the middle of something. Could I get back to you in about – minutes?'

Very few people would be offended by a response like that. Even if they are, perhaps the appropriate use of your time is more important than their momentary pique. Occasionally, saying 'No' to someone else is a small price to pay for greater effectiveness and satisfaction.

In other words, the most important way of avoiding unproductive interruptions is simply to *refuse to be interrupted*. Tell people that you're busy and that you'd be glad to talk to them later.

2. Let people know when interruptions are all right
Schedule particular blocks of time that are open for people to drop in with their concerns. Scheduling such time on your

Plan-It, and coordinating it with your secretary, is a very useful way of letting people know that they are welcome to come in with problems *during those hours*. To make it work, you must be firm about sticking to those hours.

3. *Respect other people's time*
Don't interrupt them unless absolutely necessary. By doing so, you'll send an unspoken message that you prefer not to interrupt others and accordingly that you appreciate it when others do not interrupt you.

> In the space provided, write at least one action idea you intend to apply to stop this productivity killer:

CLUTTER AND PAPERWORK

1. *Handle each piece of paper only once*
Learn to make decisions – not just postpone actions – on each letter, memo, or document you receive.

Usually you have four options:

A – act on it – now!

F – file it for future reference

R – refer it to someone else

B – bin it

Studies show that 95 per cent of material in files for one year or longer is never used. Periodically clean out files so your system stays lean and mean. You can retrieve the information you need without getting bogged down in mountains of dead files which clutter your life.

2. Learn how to 'read' a magazine (periodical, report, etc)
As you read periodicals, get in the habit of tearing out those sheets that are important to you. Set these items aside for future reference. Build a file, but *do not keep the entire original source document*. Keeping stacks of magazines simply adds to the clutter in your life.

While you are thinking about clutter and paperwork, write at least one action idea in this space that you intend to apply to stop this productivity killer:

UNPRODUCTIVE COMMUNICATION

1. Choose the right medium for your messages
Don't send a letter when a phone call will do. Don't make a call when a personal visit is needed (even if the visit takes more time and energy).

2. Obtain feedback
Even 'simple' instruction giving should be accompanied by an opportunity for feedback. Always give the person you are talking to a chance to *question* and *clarify*. Ask questions yourself to make sure things are clear. A few extra moments invested now can save hours of 'fixing' later.

3. Keep your boss appraised of your priorities
A five-minute session each day (or week) can clear the air and improve organisational productivity.

If there is a situation where your boss doesn't share your enthusiasm you can provide a brief memo explaining your activities. It could read something like this:

Dear Boss

Today I've assigned my A-1 priority to finishing the Murphy report. When that is done, I will gather the data for next week's budget sessions.

If these priorities are not consistent with what you need, please let me know. If I do not hear from you, I will assume that I'm on the right track.

A simple memo like this enhances effective communication, and provides for better direction.

Write at least one action idea in the space provided that you intend to apply to stop this productivity killer:

PROCRASTINATION
1. Use the daily priority task list you create in your planner.
2. Concentrate on doing the unpleasant (but necessary) tasks first. Get them over and enjoy the rest of the day.
3. Turn dreaded tasks into games. Compete against others or yourself. Try to beat your last effort. Play mind games.
4. Use self-discipline when all else fails (*sorry, but ultimately it may come down to that*). Provide simple rewards when you complete a difficult assignment, such as a nice meal, a film or play, a new item of clothing or a 'toy'.

Write at least one action idea in the space provided that you intend to apply to stop this productivity killer. (Do this now ... not later.)

DECISION GUIDE
When deciding how to use your time, ask:

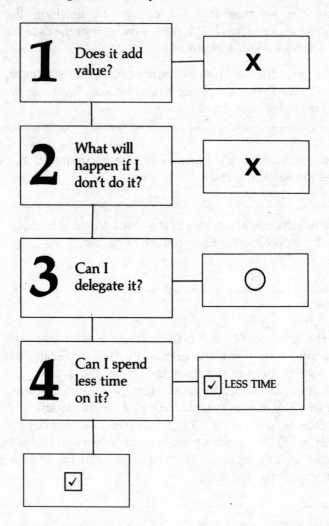

INDECISION

1. One company has as its tongue-in-cheek motto, the simple three words,

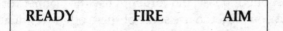

| READY | FIRE | AIM |

Sounds funny, but there's some value to that idea. Sometimes ready and fire are what we need to do. We can always adjust the aim later. Take action, *do something* and then make adjustments as necessary.

2. Make the best decision you can – BY DOING IT – and then observe your results.

3. Avoid 'perfection paralysis'. Everything you do won't be perfect, but if you start with a 'rough draft' and then shape and improve things as you go, you'll end up fine.

4. Use a decision guide like the one illustrated opposite.

5. Decide to be more decisive. Make decisions and stick to them so long as they make sense.

While you are thinking about indecision, write at least one action idea you intend to apply to stop this productivity killer:

SELF-OVERLOAD

1. Throughout this book you have been asked to focus your energy on things that are important. This concept is critical if you want to reduce the problem of self-overload.

2. Delegate all you *can* – anything others could do for you – not just what you want to.

3. Put your major effort into your value-based activities. (The other stuff isn't as important.)
4. Stay flexible. Don't become a time fanatic.

If you get out of phase and forget to use the planner for a day or two, or if you forget to use some of these other techniques, don't worry about it. Just step back and start over again. Once you develop habits of using daily tools, you'll find that you will achieve a stress-reduced balance for your life.

Don't become a time fanatic. Someone once joked that he was so programmed that when he missed a slot in a revolving door it threw him off for a whole week. Don't become a robot. Understand the nature of time and these principles of self-management but stay flexible.

> While thinking about self-overload, write at least one action idea you intend to apply to stop this productivity killer in the space provided.

Review of defences against productivity killers
Tick those which you plan to initiate action plans to combat.

- [ ] Interruptions
- [ ] Clutter and paperwork
- [ ] Unproductive communication
- [ ] Procrastination
- [ ] Indecision
- [ ] Self-overload

PART 3: A Final Thought About Balance in Your Life

Tony's story

Tony certainly looked successful. He was a young executive with a fast-growing company. His work seemed exciting. He travelled quite a bit (always first class) and earned a salary that put him in the top 10 per cent of wage earners nationally. He drove a BMW, wore what appeared to be a Rolex watch, and dressed fashionably. He seemed to be the kind of person most MBA students aspired to become. He had it made.

And he was miserable.

Under the veneer of 'success' lived an unhappy person – a man who was travelling life's fast lane with a seriously lopsided wheel. Tony's problem was one of balance.

For him, career was everything. He loved his job and dedicated himself to it with a vengeance. But after work, there wasn't much else. Tony had no regular companions away from the office. His family lived across the country; and he was a member of no community organisations, no church, no club, no 'nothing'. Because of the hours he worked he didn't engage in any hobbies or follow any exercise routine. His job was his life.

Lots of people fall into the lopsided wheel trap. We can get wrapped up with one aspect of our life (career, children, church work, community involvement, physical training, politics, etc) so deeply that nothing else is significant. We become compulsively one-sided. The last few pages of this book will talk about the importance of balance in your life.

Wellness and centring a lopsided wheel

How can we achieve a sense of wellness – a social and psychological as well as a physical sense of wellbeing? A *centred* wheel can help.

Visualise an old-fashioned wheel with spokes. If the spokes are all about the same length, the wheel is balanced. If not, a bumpy ride may be in store.

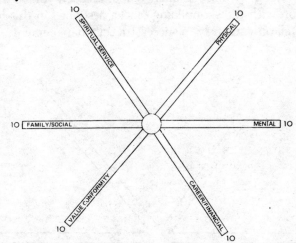

Suppose this wheel has six spokes like the one above. Each spoke represents a dimension of your life.

1. Physical
2. Mental
3. Career/Financial
4. Spiritual/Service
5. Family/Social
6. Value conformity

To decide your state of balance, assume each spoke of the wheel on page 68 is calibrated from 0 to 10. Label your six spokes and 'grade' your *degree of satisfaction* with the *progress* you are making towards value conformity. Don't expect perfection – simply measure your *progress*.

Do this for all six spokes.

Is your wheel round or lopsided?
Following the instructions on page 67, draw a line connecting the points on each spoke. Is your wheel lopsided? Is it square? Is something sticking out too far?

Redraw your wheel every month or so. By doing so, you can achieve a sense of balance – the feeling that comes from using time and resources to gain satisfaction in the six central areas that are critical to our whole personal wellness. When you do this in conjunction with the six building blocks described in this book, you are well on your way to successful self-management.

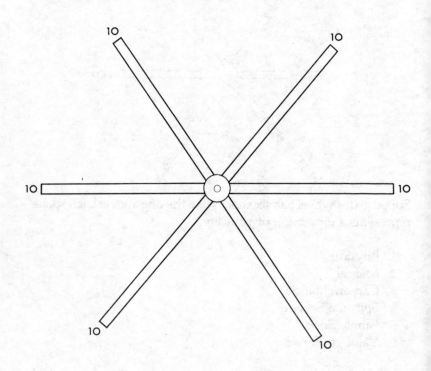

A lopsided wheel: an example

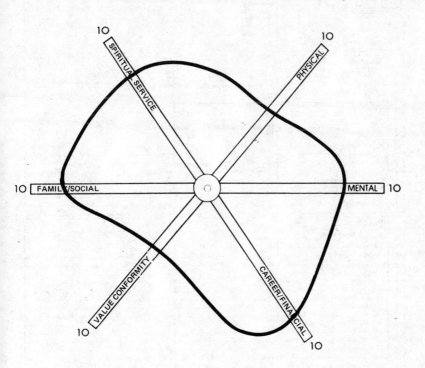

Your balance wheel

Rate the progress you are making towards conformity with your core values. Name each spoke and then rate yourself from 0 to 10. Then draw the wheel connecting your spots on each spoke. Do this every few months in a different colour ink to see what kind of progress you are making.

plan·it life organizer	Week of 19	This week	
A Must do ✓ Completed B Should do → Moved C Could do ·· Delegated ★ Urgent DO NOW ✗ Deleted			

Monday

Priority tasks	Schedule	Notes
	8	
	9	
	10	
	11	
	12	
	1	
	2	
	3	
	4	
	5	
		✓ Journal ( )

Tuesday

Priority tasks	Schedule	Notes
	8	
	9	
	10	
	11	
	12	
	1	
	2	
	3	
	4	
	5	
		✓ Journal ( )

Wednesday

Priority tasks	Schedule	Notes
	8	
	9	
	10	
	11	
	12	
	1	
	2	
	3	
	4	
	5	
		✓ Journal ( )

Thursday

	Priority tasks	Schedule	Notes
		8	
		9	
		10	
		11	
		12	
		1	
		2	
		3	
		4	
		5	
			✓ Journal □

Friday

	Priority tasks	Schedule	Notes
		8	
		9	
		10	
		11	
		12	
		1	
		2	
		3	
		4	
		5	
			✓ Journal □

Saturday

	Priority tasks	Schedule	Notes
			✓ Journal □

Sunday

	Priority tasks	Schedule	Notes
			✓ Journal □

plan·it life organizer	Month/Year	Monthly Plan				
Monday	**Tuesday**	**Wednesday**	**Thursday**	**Friday**	**Saturday**	**Sunday**

Major Tasks this Month

plan·it life organizer	Year	Yearly Plan/Record

January	February	March

April	May	June

July	August	September

October	November	December

plan·it life organiser	Year	Priority Tasks this Year

plan·it life organiser	Year		**Priority Tasks this Year**

plan·it life organizer	Life Plan
Core Values	**Value Aligning Activities**

Further Reading from Kogan Page

Better Management Skills series

Creative Thinking in Business
Delegating for Results
Effective Meeting Skills
Effective Performance Appraisals
Effective Presentation Skills
The Fifty-Minute Supervisor
How to Communicate Effectively
How to Develop a Positive Attitude
How to Develop Assertiveness
How to Motivate People
Make Every Minute Count
Memory Skills in Business
Speed Reading in Business
Successful Negotiation
Team Building

Other relevant titles:

Don't Do. Delegate! The Secret Power of Successful Managers,
    James M Jenks and John M Kelly, 1986
How to Be an Even Better Manager, 3rd edition, Michael Armstrong,
    1990
Improving Your Communication Skills, Malcolm Peel, 1990
Managing Your Time, Lothar J Seiwert, 1989

The Organised Executive, Stephanie Winston, 1989
Readymade Business Letters, Jim Dening, 1986
Readymade Business Speeches, Barry Turner, 1989
Speak With Confidence, Meribeth Bunch, 1989
Wordpower, 2nd edition, Neil Wenborn, 1990